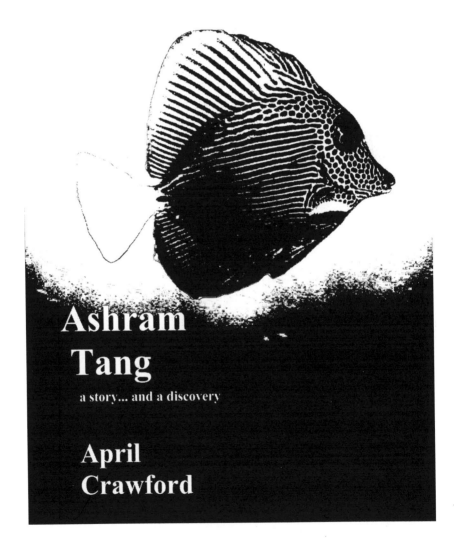

Ashram
Tang

a story... and a discovery

April
Crawford

Author: April Crawford

Publisher: Connecting Wave
   2629 Foothill Blvd.
   Unit # 353
   La Crescenta, CA 91214
   www.ConnectingWave.com

ISBN: 978-0-9823269-0-9

For Author Information: www.AprilCrawford.com

Other books via April Crawford: www.AprilCrawfordBookStore.com

"Ashram Tang", "Merka", "Toban", "Sima", "Coda" and "Connecting Wave" are trademarks.

Book Design: Allen Crawford.

Cover Painting of Ashram Tang: Dee Crawford.
www.DeeCrawfordDesigns.com

For Permissions: Publisher@ConnectingWave.com

1

It was a clear moment

above the sand. The seaweed standing tall while ripples of fluid space danced under the illuminated water rim. There was a hum that the others attributed to the rhythm of life as all of God's chosen swam to their daily routine. It was on this day that a small egg broke away from the cluster and descended down to the sandy bottom. An alarm pulsed to the others and there was dismay among the order of the Living Beings. This egg loss lamented by all would be honored. It's alleged death a tribute to those struggling to survive the depths of the sea. It was as it always was, a separation from the collective... a sure death. So it was with great surprise that a small creature returned to those who had conceived him. There was great rejoicing among the Living Beings, a miracle of sorts. A young one, who had returned from the sands, marked by tragedy, only to return as a special life. The little fish was given a special name so that all would remember the benevolence of God. His name would be Ashram, God's favorite.

So the world of the Living Beings continued without pause. Each thriving in personal endeavors and talent. All was routine in God's plans and none questioned it. Its perfection was benefiting many for eons. That is, until the day of the vision. This spiritual sighting would change forever the path of the Living Beings. This was the day God revealed himself. This was a first encounter with another dimension. The first time the Living Beings ever considered an existence other than their own. For this, Ashram would be even more singled out. This was the day Ashram saw God.

2

The universe as it was known

to Ashram extended far in many directions. It took a measurement of time to travel from one side to another. Along the way were many wonders. There was rock that pulsed with life, plants that offered nourishment and creatures that contributed to the balance of life. Ashram loved it all. He played hide & seek among the rock formations, swimming furiously with his friends around the perimeter of the universe. God provided food. It was always delicious and the sea population never missed a ceremony. The hum of existence was counted on by the Living Beings. They were masters of their environment. All were satisfied with what they knew, seeing no other way to live. This is what God had intended for them. All were thankful and all worshipped the god that took care of them. Were they not children of him? Were they not created in his image? All lived in hope of a glimpse but he was never spotted.

Ashram was happy. Whatever the will of God asked for he would submit to. He was a healthy Tang of illustrious color. Faster than his friends he abruptly crashed into the edge of the universe one-day. Stunned and shaky he reeled back into his group of friends. The lump on his head throbbing, he closed his eyes for a brief moment. When he opened them he noticed a movement not there before. He swam very still and focused on the spot right in front of him. "There!" he cried, "Did you see that?" A group of Chromis gathered about Ashram and gazed into the general direction of his fin. "We do not see anything," they said. "You are always seeing things. Perhaps you should stay still for a bit." Ashram slipped into a rest position and closed his eyes. The others thought him strange. He had always known that. It had been so since the beginning. Falling from the collective had left him a marked Living Being. One that should be observed with caution. His friends liked him but there was always that stigma that he would never lose. With his eyes still closed he found it hard to forget what he had seen. So he kept one eye open hoping to reestablish contact with whatever might have been there. Sighing, to him it appeared to be a very long wait.

3

The Living Beings

had a very simple hierarchy among them. The older ones were the guides. Knowing the perimeters of the universe was of special interest to them. There were others that coexisted with them that were of a hard shell. The enemies were wise and thoughtful. The feather dusters were elegant but not very social. There were occasional differences of opinion with the crabs, but all in all it was a harmonious existence. The population did not measure time, and had no formal written language. There was a richness of history among them as memories were passed genetically from parent to child. The primal urge for food was satisfied by the routine release of live food from the heavens. It was thought to be gift and the Living Beings absolved themselves from the eating of others by accepting God's will. Without this food they would die.

Ashram loved these rituals. The food was satisfying but he often wondered what the god looked like. Often he would ask the elders about it. Their reply was often a grunt and silence. He could not understand why they did not tell him. It took him a long time to realize that they most likely did not know. It could be the only reason for their silence. Ashram's own memory did not offer any clues either.

There was a light and dark to the existence of the Living Beings. In the light they went about their business. Searching for extra food the most prominent activity. The crabs scaled the rocks to eliminate dangerous substances. The hard shell others ate the refuse of the population. They also dissolved the remains of any Living Being that had been called to God. There were times the body would mysteriously disappear. It had been said that these bodies had been lifted up to heaven before the very eyes of witnesses. Of course Ashram had never seen this. He wished very much to have participated. His only resource came from others who claimed to have been there. Actually the witnesses were not very reliable so Ashram tended not to believe them. It was his secret desire to have it all be true. He always looked to heaven in expectation but was never satisfied.

In the dark everyone rested. The fluid surrounding them a cushion supporting them while they were not swimming.   There were reports of dark thoughts that seemed very real. It was never explained and those who had the experience rarely spoke of it. Dark thoughts led to a separation form the true reality. Ashram had thoughts in the dark but they were never unpleasant. In them he was a super living being. One who had knowledge of the whole universe, he was no longer plagued by unanswerable questions. He knows it all, the mysteries, the legends and the opening to heaven.   Ashram never spoke of his thoughts. What would be the use? He would be shunned even more than he already was. It was simply not worth it. So his thoughts turned to dreams while he rested. And in those moments he could swim and never touch the edges of the universe.   God would show himself and the mysteries of the universe would unfold before him.

In the light everything was different. The other life forms responded by blooming larger. There was a hum of energy that resounded while it sent ripples of energy through the fluid space. Ashram inhaled deeply by raising his fins. The rush of fluid was energizing him to move even faster among the rocks. Everything was alive. The pulse entering his body was almost a spiritual experience.

Truly God would speak to him someday. Ashram felt special even while the others taunted him. As he darted among the rocks he closed his eyes trying to visualize the world of God. Of course he never shared these moments with the others. Only his best friend Merka knew bits and pieces of what Ashram really thought. The rest all thought him strange. Everyone knew that God would never reveal himself. Wasn't it enough that he caused the dark and light? Did he not send food from the heavens so that they could all eat? Was he merciful and loving so that they all could be born? And the old to die peacefully? Why did Ashram have to ask such stupid questions? Ashram never thought his questions were stupid. He believed that someday he would see God. Of course he kept that to himself.

4

No one ever spoke of the time

the egg dropped to the sands. No one ever revealed that Ashram was the one returned from the dead. He was different but he was never sure why. The elders thought it prudent not to burden the young Tang with that knowledge. It was obvious that the fall had severed the mental link shared by the Living Beings. They could not tap into Ashram's mind. He was an individual through and through. They hoped he would blend into the collective life and that he would lose the taint of singularity. In their universe the plural mind was essential for existence. Individual personality existed but the mass consciousness created and maintained this universe. The elders knew it. The worry of Ashram's predicament would be watched. He had already displayed unusual talents the young ones would understand as they matured. All hoped that Ashram would become one of them. They would be wrong. The bump on the sandy floor would allow Ashram a different vision. The others would never understand his thoughts and experiences. He could tell them but they would never experience it. This began immediately but was ignored. They hoped it would go away. Again they were wrong.

Ashram had one friend to call his own. His name was Merka. He was rather plain but made up for it with his quick mind. Ashram and Merka spent a lot of time together. Hungry for attention, Merka followed him around constantly and adored him for his support. He was a gray Chromis rather bland in appearance. His love for Ashram made up for it all.

No one marked the day Ashram and Merka began to get into trouble. It seemed like the problems were eternal only beginning a moment ago. All would have been well if they had kept the incident to themselves, however, Ashram was unable to contain himself. And Merka in his love for Ashram backed his story completely. It was doubtful Merka saw anything but his support of Ashram sent ripples through the entire universe of the Living Beings.

Out for a morning swim, Ashram had stopped abruptly at the edge of the universe. Merka thought the pause was merely to rest. After a few moments of stillness Merka nudged his friend hoping to move him along. He was anxious to complete the excursion and begin looking for food. Ashram, however, seemed transfixed. Looking into nothing his eyes wide with surprise, he moved right into the walls of the universe. Merka became alarmed when he heard Ashram say "Wait! Who are you? Are you a god?" Knowing that the Living Beings would sense what Ashram was saying, Merka began to butt him from behind. His hope was to wake him up and to move on with their swim. Alas, it was not to be. Ashram stared into the nothingness. He abruptly turned to Merka and exclaimed, "I saw God! I just saw God!" Merka's first reaction was to place his fin over Ashram's mouth. Surely he had just gone mad! Struggling together, Merka pulled Ashram from the edge. With one mighty tug the two fish tumbled over each other until they were tangled in seaweed.

Ashram was laughing and wiggling his tail fin. He was more excited than he had ever been. "Oh Merka! Did you see it?! I saw a magnificent creature. I'm sure it was God! It smiled right at me! Oh Merka, I'm sure there is a God!"

5

Merka hugged his friend
and sighed. Truly Ashram was mad. The others would
never believe him. It would be up to him to protect his
friend. Although he had seen nothing he replied, "Oh yes,
was he not beautiful? Let's get out of here before we
anger God." With that he tugged at Ashram hoping to
move away from the edge. To his dismay Ashram
continued to stare into nothingness. Merka knew that this
was not going to go away. His friend was truly out of his
mind. With a sigh he swam around Ashram and waited.

The sight of what he thought was God froze Ashram
in the moment. All that he had ever known flashed before
him while blending into the vision he beheld. Therefore
he took many moments before he dared expel the water in
his gills. When he did it was ever so gently. Nothing
could disturb the being. It had appendages like a crab,
only not so many. There were facial features unfamiliar to
Ashram. What were most noticeable were the eyes. They
seemed to look right into his own. Was this God? If so the
Living Beings were certainly not made in his image. He

tried to tell Merka to be quiet.   He knew he was unresponsive but he wanted the vision to continue.

Becoming bold in the moment, Ashram swam to the edge of the universe. In an instant the being put one of its appendages to where the universe should have ended. It was an ugly tentacle with several pieces attached to the end. Surely this was not God. He began to hear a subtle vibration as the hole in the face began to move. Was it trying to communicate with him? Surely if it were God it would just send him a mental message.   Ashram shuddered and moved away. Perhaps this was not God, but what was it? There was movement that became blurry and the image began to dissolve. The tightness in his head began to subside and Ashram found himself once again with his friend. Merka was circling him in distress. What should he tell him?

Merka knew something had happened. He tried to tap into Ashram'.s consciousness but as usual was unable to do so.   So he started talking out of worry and discomfort. His biggest hope was that his friend would tell him what had happened in those few brief moments.

6

The hum of life continued

as the two friends gazed at each other. They both knew that whatever came next would change their friendship forever. Ashram was the first to ripple the water. He knew that Merka wanted to be included. He could not hold back from him the vision he had witnessed. There was something out there. If not God, another life form. The connection was irreversible. Could it be God? If it was then something truly holy had occurred. If not, then the universe was not defined as the Living Beings supposed. Either way, Ashram knew he had to let the collective mind know. Merka felt a slight twinge in his stomach as his friend began to talk. The rest of them would be skeptical but Merka knew he would stand by his friend regardless of what everyone thought.

Ashram pushed up against the edge of the universe straining to see more. He swam all the way to the top, then meticulously slid to the sandy bottom. Nothing. All was as it always was. Merka suggested that they return to the rocks to think. Ashram knew that he was right but was reluctant to leave. Just one more glimpse would fill his heart with joy. With a final sigh they both turned home. By now the others would have an idea what had happened to them. It was time to face the music.

7

THE ELDERS

Sima the Crab

Sima the crab was exhausted.
He spent his days scaling the rocks for parasites and food. Changes in the atmosphere were polluting his world at a rapid pace. It was with great determination that he went about his business. Without him they would all die. He knew it but the others were either too stupid or too self absorbed to notice. The collective mind was amusing to him. He was part of it but his species had evolved to a new level where he could block their inquisitive minds. He was not really interested in them anyway. Long ago he had stopped trying to refocus them on anything outside of their created universe. The curse of intelligence his alone to bear, but most of the time he was able to endure. The self-imposed singleness of his existence. There were no others like him. He had legs while the others swam around in circles... doing the same thing over and over. Accepting his fate and position was something of which he was most proud. By scaling the rocks he had learned to focus his thought. In doing so evolution had allowed him

to know that there was more. He had not actually viewed anything. He just "knew." His patience in scavenging served his patience in waiting. Waiting for the coming of God. Well if not God, then the Beings just on the other side of the universe edge. They were there.

So it was with great interest that he awaited the arrival of the Tang. "I have seen God," cried the Tang. "So you have," whispered Sima to himself.

8

Toban the Shrimp Master

Toban was of a great species. Centuries of history played out before him. He was a slight fellow by shrimp standards. His base was outward similar to Sima. The tough shell exterior protecting his inner parts. He considered himself superior in many ways. The magnificent intellect he possessed was only enhanced by the past life memories he retained. Only the crab came close. His guidance was sought after, his knowledge beneficial in crisis, and his ability to clean up after the Living Beings priceless. The main difference between the crab and the shrimp was ego. Toban's was much larger and consequently harder to feed. Natural tendencies to consume the dead provided a unique service. Over the years Toban ingested many of the Living Beings upon their death. There was no God as far as he was concerned, just natural process. He believed that once you were dead that was it. There was nothing. Anything else the collective mind thought were fantasies designed to ward-away nightmares. He stopped trying to explain this years ago.

Toban believed his species was the only true one. The memory of other lives a gift but also a burden. He would remember his death when he awakened in a new body. It wasn't a pleasant thought but a natural one. He accepted it as the way things were. There was a true feeling for the other Living Beings but in the end he found them all to be incredibly boring. Even in the collective they had no comprehension of the deepness of his thoughts. His place on the elders' council was an honor but his impatience with all their petty dramas was annoying. So on this day he was surprised to feel the presence of a familiar movement. These flashes were few and far between. It was spiritual in its content. The resounding "I have seen God" rippled endlessly to the ends of the universe. Looking over the rocks he was even more surprised to see the source. A Tang? A Tang had seen God? Toban did not think so. He did, however, hoist himself over the rocks to reach the center of the conclave just as the Tang skidded to a stop in the center of the circle.

9

The Reverend

The living Beings were intelligent, but their perception of themselves was limited. They perceived the world in a conglomerate single-minded fashion. Rules were set forth and they followed. Ideas were established and categorized. Everyone had a function and they fulfilled it. No one remembered why these things were so. They were just accepted and that was that. Of course there was a leader to whom they all pledged allegiance, an acknowledged superior species. He was a Living Being but more, as the days could be marked by his approach. There was an ethereal aura about him. And why not? He was an ordained minister of God. Gifted with the sight since birth, he was able to communicate one on one with the creator. His name was Coda. He was a cardinal. All the beauty in God's eye manifested itself in the form of this being. Unlike the others there was a glide and rhythm in his movement. All wanted to emulate him.

Coda thought himself to be the right hand of God. He was a righteous soul and truly believed in the existence of God. His power caused him to feel inadequate inside. There were those who believed he had seen God. This used to alarm Coda in the early days of his service. The stories of him having the second sight were grossly over exaggerated. At one time he tried to dispel the rumors. It had happened when he was very young. He had been playing with some friends and swam too close to the black square that hung in the sky. It supplied the much-needed ripple effect necessary to sustain life. Being a stubborn cardinal, he ignored the warnings of the collective minds and did it any way. In his folly he was sucked into the black box before the alarmed faces of his friends. They were all sure he was dead.

Coda, on the other hand, was having a strange dream. He was floating in darkness. There was no fear. An odd sound kept repeating. Coda was lulled by the rhythm and relaxed against the sides. "This must be what it is like to die," he thought. "It's not so bad." With that he allowed the dream to completely take over. He remembered a fleshy appendage coming towards him. It released him from the box. In his dream he began to spiral down to the sandy bottom of his well Known Universe. He abruptly awakened when he bumped into a rock. Shaken, he hovered in the moment.

By this time the entire body of the Living Beings had come to the rescue. Instead of a dead cardinal, they found him posed by the rocks. There were calmative sighs of rejoice before his mother promptly slapped him with her tail fin. All of them could feel his experience. They, however, could not understand the depth of it. They thought it had all been a dream... a dream that God had provided. Coda was not sure what happened but decided to use it to his advantage. He embellished his thoughts to keep himself out of more trouble. He was not certain any of the events had happened. All he knew was that the penetrating eyes of the Livings Beings were upon him. So he decided to confirm that he had seen God. They believed him.

Now on this morning many eons later, Coda was enjoying his status. The experience so long ago faded somewhat but ever present in his on going popularity contest within the community. He had a good thing going. His dream a secret he withheld so that he could be who he was now. He was doing God's work, wasn't he? Coda always thought so... that is until that cursed little Tang came swimming into the center of the circle screaming he had seen God.

10

The Community

The center of the community was not a particular place. It pulsed with the rhythm of the collective mind. There was always a gathering that became the village center whenever one of the collectives had something to say. It was usually the elders who convened the meetings either to deliver information or warnings. Everyone, though connected mentally, usually went about his or her own business. Whispers among the Living Beings were common to Ashram. Ever since he had been young there was rumor about the truth of his survival. Ashram knew that he was an oddity. No one had ever returned after separating from the egg cluster. He had no memory of the event but the glances and whisperings among the others had become routine to him.

The collective mind of the Living Beings did not function to eliminate privacy. It was a selective process used for spiritual purposes. Daily communication was verbal. Not all information was shared continually with the whole. It was rather like a feeling or impulse. On this day, however, the exuberant Ashram startled his counterparts. They all knew immediately something was up. It was Ashram who needed to clarify what that was.

Ashram slid to a stop, his eyes wide with anticipation. "I saw something!" he cried, pointing his fin in the general direction. "It was only for a moment, but it was there. I swear!"

There was a ripple of nervousness among the crowd. What could the young Tang have seen? His reputation alone was enough to discredit him. No one spoke as he continued. "I'm telling you, there was something at the end of the universe! I think it was God!" A gasp from the crowd stopped Ashram from continuing. They did not believe him. The eyes of disbelief enveloped him. Tentacles of contempt began to choke him as he looked from one face to another. Looking for any ally, Ashram searched frantically for any hope of acceptance. There was none. Only Merka hovered at his side. He had not spoken at all. Surly he had seen something! Ashram turned to Merka, his eyes pleading with him to agree with his story. "You saw it didn't you?" pleaded Ashram.

"Ah well, maybe," replied Merka. His loyalty to his friend frayed as the eyes of the crowd looked upon him.

Before anymore could be said there was a comment from Sima. He never spoke unless provoked. His anti establishment status set him apart from the others. Ashram felt the air go out of his soul's knowing. Sima would never believe him. So it was with great astonishment that he looked into Sima's eyes. "Let us go see for ourselves." said Sima "Perhaps the Tang is correct, perhaps he is not. With that Sima crawled through the crowd to the end of the universe. The Living Beings following quietly behind. Only Coda lagged behind the group, worrying that his own universe was about to be destroyed.

11

The Edge of the Universe

Out of breath and excited, Ashram could hardly contain himself… his desire to speak hindered by the lack of air. His mind was whirling with so many thoughts. Now that he had everyone's attention the impact of what was about to happen hit him square in the face. Swallowing, he glanced at all the faces before him. Any friendly face would give him the encouragement he needed. The last face at the end of the crowd was Sima. His eyes flickered with interest and a smile danced on his mouth. It was this brief exchange that spurred Ashram to speak. With a deep breath he stammered. "I saw something. I think it was God. It was right over here."

There, it was said. The murmuring of the crowd was not distinct enough for Ashram to feel any indication of what they were thinking. Some were uncertain of what he said. Some were sure he was insane, while others felt pity for the poor Tang. Obviously the blow to his head had damaged him long ago. As the individual thoughts were expressed, Ashram felt himself getting angry. They did not understand.   Sima raised his claw and asked for silence.

All eyes turned to the crab.   The silence was deafening as Sima moved forward.   Sima was still an awkward moment as far as the Living Beings were concerned.   To have legs that provided mobility was a foreign concept they all still had trouble with.   Most averted their eyes as he made his way through the crowd. He was respected but still considered an oddity.   Sima knew this but in his experience no longer cared what they thought.   Someone needed to stand by the Tang.

Sima was a wise being.   To hear confirmation of his own suspicions filled him with new energy.   Perhaps this Tang had seen what he had always suspected.   There were other Beings in the universe.   Things that were so foreign that the Living Beings would consider them gods.   Why hell! Maybe they were gods!   Sima surely wanted to find out.   This was the most exciting moment he had ever known.   Suddenly he was no longer exhausted.   A new pulse of energy flowed through him.   As he grew closer to the Tang he felt almost a spiritual awakening.   Oh God!

This is what he had waited for his whole life. Face to face with Ashram he extended his claw and cried, "Behold, this Tang has seen something. Perhaps the creator of all! Listen and learn my fellow Beings. We are at the cusp of the divine."

With that statement Ashram immediately fainted.

Ashram Disappears

12

Ashram in his stress floated to the top of the rocks. There was a hush among the Living Beings. The closed eyes and limp fins were a clear indicator that Ashram was dead. Alas! Now they would never know for sure if what he said was true. No one would ever be special enough to be like him. Sima stared up at his body. Disappointment hovered in every crevice. He turned to Merka and said, "Do you know where he was when he saw this vision?" Merka, up to now speechless, struggled to find his voice. All he could do was to stare into the eyes of the crab. There was something scary and different about him. Never before had he even noticed Merka was alive. And now he decided that he did not want to talk to Sima. Abruptly he swam away leaving Sima clinging to a rock. Toban moved along side of him and waited. "I don't think he's dead." Sima waved him away with his claw. "We'll never know will we? If only he had not been cut off from the collective, we would be able to feel his life force. Most likely, he is dead."

"Think what you will," replied Toban. "He's not dead." With that Toban turned back to the rocks. One eye ever watchful for the return of the Tang.

Soon all the Living Beings returned to their daily routines. There was no more talk of God. Those who see God always die. Just look what happened to the Tang? No more visions for any of them. Coda retained his place of spiritual leader. Let him be the only who had seen God and lived. They would stick to this place of reality. All were in agreement. All that is except Toban… and possibly Sima.

13

Juliet

The sun flowed through the lace curtains and danced upon the upturned nose of Juliet. She hated her nose for it always gave her that "cute" label by all of her relatives. She was a precocious child of ten years. Doted upon by her family, she excelled in academics and music. Ever inquisitive, she found everything about life exciting. She was an only child of well-to-do parents. It was no surprise that she inherited their fair looks and blue eyes. They sparkled when she laughed, revealing a tinsel mouth of corrective braces. She had had them for exactly eighteen months and three days, and according to her orthodontist, she had exactly eighteen months and four days to go. Precisely. Precision was a favorite of Juliet's. Her favorite subject was math. She liked exactly two tablespoons of sugar in her mom's homemade lemonade. She liked all of her clothes to match perfectly. All of her hobbies and toys were of a precise nature.

When Juliet was five years old her father bought her a salt-water tank. Together they adapted the environment and began a collection of exotic fish. The exacting measure required for a balanced tank fascinated Juliet. She and her dad spent hours balancing the environment, so that every creature had a chance to live. Every Saturday they made a field trip to the store to purchase another fish. Juliet delighted in choosing the fish. Salt-water tanks provided for some very colorful and exotic fish and Juliet's dad always let her pick. Over the past few years the population had grown quite a bit. There was even an attempt at breeding that was somewhat successful. Some of the eggs had separated but with diligent care some had survived. Well maybe just one, but it was better than nothing was. Juliet had stayed up very late waiting for the egg to fertilize and transform. By some miracle it had even risen back to the collective. And turned into a promising little Tang.

Juliet and her dad made the fish tank a full time project. Over the past few years they had seen some fish come and go but the little Tang had survived much to the delight of Juliet.

For her sixth birthday her Dad gave her a little crab. She named him Sima. He was necessary to the tank to eat bacteria but Juliet found him to be most entertaining. She could swear that he looked right into her eyes as he foraged the rocky sides of the tank. Often she tapped gently on the glass hoping he would recognize her. She wished she could to talk to him, his little claws ferociously shoving bits of algae into his mouth.

Everyday was a new adventure with Sima. She never knew where he would be in the tank. It seemed he played a unique game of hide and seek with Juliet. She always found him some new place.

On her seventh birthday her parents presented her with a shrimp. Different than the others, his precise manipulations of his surroundings enchanted Juliet. Her connection with him not as strong as with Sima. She did, however, gaze at him everyday. She was not sure but she supposed that he had eaten several of the fish that died when there was a miscalculation of chemicals in the tank. She named him Toban but she knew he would never understand how much he meant to her. Both creatures were her favorites because of their differences.

Juliet wished on occasion that she could hug her universe of sea creatures. Knowing that it was impossible, she consoled herself pressing her face as close to the glass as she could. "Maybe, just maybe some day they will know that I am here," she thought. With that Juliet curled up next to the tank and placed her hand on the glass, just as the little Tang floated up.

14

The Meeting

Ashram felt weightless as he floated to the top of the tank. All of his surroundings blurred into a single image. Upside down, he managed again to see the image of God. It peered at him expectantly as it moved its appendages in some sort of pattern. For a brief instant he believed he had died. If only he could move he would stride purposely to meet his God. Alas, he found himself unable to adjust himself to a respectable swim stance. He floated helplessly, belly up, to the sky. How embarrassing! If this were the great meeting, he would have preferred to be upright. In vain, he attempted to right himself. Too late he saw an object coming towards him. Truly he was dead and this thing was about to remove him from everything he had ever known. He closed his eyes tightly, the tension in every scale of his body apparent.

Juliet became alarmed as she saw the Tang floating towards the top of the tank. She maintained the chemical balance with utmost precision. If a fish was dying she wanted to know why. The Tang's eyes were open, the mouth sucking water, why was it dying? Juliet reached for a net. Obviously the Tang needed inspection. Gently she slipped the net around the fish. As she brought it closer to the surface she was surprised to see it looking her squarely in the eyes. Gently she brushed a finger down its scaly sides. There was no apparent damage. Its eyes so alert seemed to look at her expectantly. "Hi little fella! Are you okay?" she inquired.

Ashram felt paralyzed in the moment. This God had some sort of mouth that moved. There was no sound. However, he could feel a slight vibration as the mouth made different patterns. Was God speaking to him? Oh, he really hoped the others were watching. Looking down he noticed them all oblivious to his situation. It figured. Here he was in the circle of God and they were all having a regular day. No one would ever believe him. They would chalk it up to his early injuries and call him a fool. Ashram closed his eyes and wished with all his might for a miracle. When he opened them the god was smiling. Somehow he felt safe. In that instant he up righted himself and looked into the eyes of God.

"Hello, little fellow, are you okay?" said God.

Ashram blinked once and replied, "Yeah, I guess so."

Neither being said a word. The thoughts of one species blended with another. Truly a miracle. More than either of them would ever know.

Juliet was concerned that the little Tang was dying. She was sure that the chemical balance of the tank was fine. There was no evident reason for the fish to be floating belly up to the top of the tank. Upon closer inspection, one could see the gills moving. It was in trouble but not necessarily dying. Juliet scooped the fish up and placed him in a special tank. It was here that she attempted to revive ill or injured fish. Gently, she released Ashram into the water. There were no obvious wounds or marks of illness. With her face pressed against the glass she dropped some antibiotics into the tank. With a little patience and time, perhaps she could save this little guy. In the past she had never been successful when one of her fish became ill. It was an ongoing project of hers to "treat" them. Her father often chided her for the zeal with which she went about her task. The let down when she failed was debilitating. Juliet, however, was beginning to realize that sometimes things just died. All she could do was care for the fish and hope for the best.

Ashram opened his eyes but remained very still and upside down. His environment felt different. For the first time he did not hear the hum of the collective. The silence making him feel very alone was overwhelming. The sound of the one voice echoing through him, "Are you all right little guy?" becoming a mantra that kept him sane in the silence. Opening one eye he knew that his response was out loud, but to whom had he spoken? The Living Beings of his universe disappeared in a vacuum of something he had never experienced. The question answered in his own voice....."I guess so"........ floating away from him in ripples. Per chance he was dead. Then why could he still feel so alive? Per chance he was insane and his universe now becoming an asylum from which he would never escape. Opening the other eye he found himself staring into the eyes of the god he had envisioned.

Did God want to know of his safety? Sucking down a gulp of funny feeling water he mustered up his courage. Juliet was certain she heard someone speak.

She looked around the bedroom surprised to see that no one was there. Often her mom would peek in on her while she did homework, but the door was firmly closed. She was alone. Her attention went back to the aquarium. The Tang had flipped back over and was swimming around. It looked as if he was all right after all. Just to be sure, Juliet decided to keep him in the other tank at least overnight. He was one of her favorites, a beautiful shade of purple that turned yellow at the tail. She remembered that she had almost lost him once before when he had split off from the other Tang eggs. It was odd because eventually all of the others had died and he had survived. Surely he was special. Looking again closely in to the tank she observed the Tang looking directly into her eyes. Again she heard the voice… "Are you God?"

With her hand to her mouth, Juliet thought "Oh my God, he's talking to me!"

Ashram was ecstatic! The being before him had responded. Obviously it needed to put its appendage over its mouth to communicate. It had exclaimed, "He's talking to me!" Before that it had identified itself as "My God." This was too good to be true. Here he was, crazy Ashram looking into the eyes of God and really talking to him. With anticipation Ashram swam closer. It appeared that he was in some sort of bubble. There were boundaries but yet he could see clearly. Hopefully God would speak to him again.

Juliet sat quietly while she pondered what to do. The Tang's eyes were still inquiring. How does one talk to a fish? She spoke the words, "I'm Juliet" and there was no response. She tried again by just *thinking* the words. Very faintly she heard "Juliet the God". It repeated over and over until it became very loud. The Tang swam in circles but never took its eyes from hers. The fish was definitely talking to her. Juliet became transfixed in front of the tank. Her mind a swirl of questions and answers. Suddenly she realized that she needed to simplify her sentences. The Tang abruptly stopped swimming and said, "I'm Ashram." His mouth did not move but the thoughts transferred directly to Juliet.

15

Sima could not concentrate.
For days he had been hard at work taking the algae off the rocks. His usual precision was hindered by the fact he could not get his mind off the Tang. All of the others had gone on with their existences without so much as a backward glance. Their daily dramas consuming their every movement. Not so for Sima. He was sure that the Tang was still alive. The voicing of that opinion he knew was useless with the general population. However, he guessed that Toban had his doubts also. Of course neither of them had voiced their opinions to anyone... especially to each other.

Sima knew of other places. He had glimpsed them in his mind many times. While scavenging the rocks he had plenty of time for quiet meditation. It was here that the other realms had been revealed. He wasn't sure if they were projections of his own mind or actual divine revelations. He just knew that they were valid in some form.

Today he stared out onto the horizon. He wondered where Ashram really was. Could there be a god that revealed itself to the Tang? Was he a benevolent god? Sima wished he had been the one to have this real vision. Perhaps the others would have accepted it more from him. After all, he was regarded as a sage to the Living Beings. Hoping to talk to Toban would be futile. They had not had a civil conversation in years. And besides he was a shrimp. It was common knowledge that crabs were more evolved than shrimp. Even God knew that!

16

Toban & Merka

Toban was bored.
The daily grind was getting to him. A little excitement was in order. He thought that excitement might come from the feisty little Tang. What was his name? Astro? Abraham? Ashram? Yes, that was it, Ashram. Ashram had provided the only real energy in the universe for quite some time. Toban really hoped that he had seen God. What a ray of hope that possibility had been. A hope dashed as the Tang floated up, dead as could be. Toban was so disappointed. He wondered what was going through Sima's mind. Perhaps he should go speak with him. No, that was probably a bad idea. Sima would not speak with him. Or if he did, it would only prove to be insulting. No, he would just let it go. The Tang was dead and that was that.

Merka was despondent, realizing his best friend was dead. His heart aching in disbelief, he swam aimlessly. Ashram was so special. And because Merka had hung out with him, he was special by association. Now that was gone. Merka now had to deal with his mediocrity. He returned to the place that Ashram had seen God. Straining his eyes he stared relentlessly into the horizon. Nope, no God, just the universe as far as he could see. Without Ashram he felt incredibly lonely. His depression mounting, Merka decided to do the only thing he could do. He would swim to the edge of the universe and kill himself. With a gulp of unrealized bravery he began the journey. Faster and faster he swam, the edge of his demise coming to meet him. The edge so very near now. Merka closed his eyes and prepared for the end. One can only imagine his surprise when he plowed right into the invisible wall. He did not die. The goose bump on his head merely scrambled his thoughts as he realized the universe was not what he thought.

17

Ashram

Ashram swam to the sand hoping to ground himself. Brushing a fin against the gravel he reveled in the sifting of so many pieces of the universe regarded as home. Closing his eyes the pictures of his existence filled him. The briefest moments etched in his memory provided comfort. Each intersection with that he lived, giving credence to the life he lived. Burrowing back and forth Ashram connected with the essence of the life he had created. It was real. It was comforting. When he opened his eyes he expected the vision of God to have disappeared, blending into a vision created by his over exuberant psyche. Instead he opened his eyes to a tentacle brushing the sand beside him, while the god smiled brightly on the other side of the universe. It was not a vision. It was real. The god was reaching toward him.

The tentacle brushed lightly against his skin. It was oddly warm. The ends were covered in a sort of shell. He could have related it to an octopus but there were only five tentacles. The eyes are what disturbed Ashram. They were imploring. The vibrations of its communication clear as a bell. The mixing of verbal frequencies somehow making sense. If he closed his eyes he could almost make out coherent communication. The word "Hello!" becoming most clear. Would a god just say "hello"? He had already embarrassed himself by claiming to have spotted God, how could he tell them that God had spoken? "And just what did God have to say?" they would ask. Ashram knew that the answer would be important. Therefore he decided to listen carefully. The levels of vibration were taking on a pattern. Perhaps he would be able to convey a message. "What a cute little fish you are!" remarked the god. Ashram gulped and was astonished. The god had spoken and it sounded favorable.

Juliet pressed her face closer to the glass. The little Tang stared wide-eyed back at her. She shook her head slightly, sure that her eyes were deceiving her. The Tang was aware of her presence and was communicating with her. Juliet held her breath and moved her hand back and forth across the glass. The Tang mimicked the motion.

Not knowing what to do, she moved slowly away to get her camera. She was going to need proof.

Ashram slowly withdrew his fin. The god had responded, the moment was finished but the repercussions would stay with him forever. He had witnessed God and God had acknowledged him. It was too beautiful for words. From the looks of it heaven was a strange place. It looked fluid but movement was not the same. The god did not hover but took jerky movements in its environment. Ashram could not wait to tell Sima, Toban and the others.

18

The Others

They would surely think him mad now.
He thought of Sima. He would go to him first. With his
lack of proof he could think of no other to approach. If
only there were some way to prove it. The god was
moving about the edges of the universe. Its face, though
strange, seemed harmless enough. Suddenly it came to
him. He would bring Sima here. And perhaps Toban
would come too. Without further thought Ashram swam
to the rocks.

Juliet & Ashram

"Oh, don't swim away!" cried Juliet. She had just
found her camera and was ready to take a shot. The little
Tang was descending to a rocky cove out of sight. If she
wasn't quick enough he may stay in that area for who
knew how long? Tapping on the side of the tank she tried
to lure him back. Disappointed, Juliet sat on the edge of
her bed. The Tang had already disappeared.

Juliet was sorry she had not kept him in the sick tank. There, he would have been more accessible. Pressing her face against the glass, Juliet tried to see between the rocks.

Ashram hovered close to the vivid coral rocks. Hoping to shield himself from the god, he tried to blend in with the rocks. He realized he was once again on his home turf. This meant he must get to Sima and Toban as soon as he could. Peering around the corner, he waited for the chance to slip away.

Sima was just finishing a day if scavenging. His legs were cramped by the long hours of hanging upside down. His claws were sore from clipping away at the rocks. All he wanted to do was slide into his dark habitat to sleep. Having just jumped to the sandy surface, he prepared to rest. He could hardly wait. So it was with great irritation that he viewed the resurrection of that bothersome Tang called "Ashram".

Sima & Ashram

19

The little guy came over there again with yet another story of gods and universes. Would he never give up? He was supposed to be dead, wasn't he? All of the Living Beings had seen him ascend to heaven. Seen it with their own eyes! Why Sima had been there too! Perhaps this was a vision or nightmare. Living Beings just didn't come back from the dead. With a sigh, Sima waited until Ashram had caught up with him. Out of breath the Tang began another outrageous story. "Sima! It's me Ashram!" cried Ashram.

Rolling his eyes, Sima acknowledged him.

"Yes Ashram, it is indeed yourself. What is it this time? And are you not dead?" said Sima.

"Oh, I am not dead, quite the contrary. I have seen something extraordinary. God is alive and she is a female."

"Are you sure it is a god?" asked Sima.

"I am not sure what she is. She is not a Living Being. That is all I know."

Sima counted the moments before he spoke again. Toban must be included in this conversation. Both he and Toban knew a day like this would come. Now that it was here, together they needed to face the future. God had appeared and nothing would be the same again. Sima sighed and told the Tang, "Come with me. We need to see Toban. Then we will decide what needs to be done."

Ashram was not sure what the crab meant but he followed meekly to the shrimp's lair.

Toban was not in a receptive mood. He had eaten something that had disagreed with him. It was screaming its way through his digestive tract and causing him discomfort. All he really wanted to do was hang upside down under the rocks, that position always relieved him on such occasions. He saw Sima and the Tang approaching. Wasn't the Tang supposed to be dead?

Incredibly, there he was following behind the crotchety old crab. Surely no good was to come of any conversation with them. Toban wished he had had time to hide. Whatever they wanted he knew that they expected his help. The thought made him even more nauseous. The resurrection of the Tang would need to be explained to the rest of the Living Beings. And God knew where the Tang had been. Closing his eyes, Toban tried to imagine himself away from the impending conversation. He was not successful.

"Toban my friend!" exclaimed Sima. "We are in need of your wisdom."

Turning to Sima, Toban replied, "Of course you are. Every time there is a crisis I turn into everyone's best friend."

"This is a matter of great urgency," replied Sima.

"Yes, yes, the resurrection of the Tang's big news. Pray tell young Tang. Have you been with God, and if so, why have you returned to this wretched place? I would think one would rather be with the gods."

"Ah sir, you see, uh, well it's like…" said Ashram.

"Come lad, spit it out. Are you participating in some sort of fraud?" said Toban.

Sima, becoming agitated, turned to Toban. "Look, you old insect, this youngster has a fantastic story. He says it is true and I believe him. If you have become narrow in your perception of the universe then so be it. We will take our story elsewhere and leave you out of it."

"Wait, wait, wait," replied Toban. "I was only testing the boy. One has to be sure before treading unknown waters. You and I both sense the existence of another place. The others however are oblivious. We cannot have a foolish Tang giving false testimony. If the story is true then it will hold up under scrutiny."

Turning to Ashram with an evil eye, he said, "So Tang, tell me your story and I will determine what is to be done."

Turning to Sima he said, "if the story rings true, I will stand behind the boy. Know however, I have heard many stories… stories of fancy, that is. I require some sort of proof. So begin your story Tang, and we will see if you are worthy of the attention of an old shrimp and crab."

20

The Shrimp & Crab

The Shrimp and the Crab listened to the story of the Tang. Each moment was filling them with much excitement. Both had had dreams about such an encounter. Ideas that were on the cusp of their perception only to slide away in the actual reality. Sima felt himself becoming emotional and struggled to gain control. All of his pre-supposed ideas about his universe were true. There were other places of existence. Places so very different from the one he lived in. Glancing at Toban he knew the shrimp was sharing the experience. When their eyes met they were filled with wonder. The Tang was telling the truth. No physical proof was needed. Now what to do.

Coda should be told. After all, he was the designated leader of the Living Beings. He should be present if they decided to go see this god for themselves. He had claimed to have had a similar experience. Perhaps he would be helpful.

Toban decided to fetch Coda, then perhaps the four of them could go see for themselves. Sima argued that it could not be a god. At least not like the others had thought. He would bide his time, however. Let them think what they liked. His sensing was always true. This was a creature from another plane of existence. That simple.

Coda was a busy fellow. His control over the Living Beings was limited and wrought only through manipulation. He had created quite a position for himself and clung to it greedily. He was not pleased to see Toban and the others approaching. It could only mean trouble. He took a strong stance and waited. Toban was not easily fooled. It would take all of his might to deter the shrimp from what he was intending. With a gulp he faced the shrimp.

"What do you want?" asked Coda.

"You," said Toban. "I need your presence for a very pressing matter. Please come with me."

"This could only lead to trouble," thought Coda. How could he get out of it? He turned to the trio and smiled. It was a million-dollar smile that had attained the leadership position among the Living Beings. He was the one they looked up to. His wisdom often guiding individuals into productive lives. It was what Coda had always strived for, the adoration of the masses. In his universe, he was God. In charge and in control of his mantra for existing. He too had inklings of something else. It was very small in nature and his huge ego often dismissed the feeling. However, Coda knew there was more. He simply denied the possibility because his own position would be threatened. The shrimp and the crab had always irritated him. Their self-superiority contest annoyed him even more. Inside he knew they were wise and correct about a lot of things. Coda just did not want to admit it.

21

Evil in the Universe

Gazing at their smug faces and the presence of the Tang made his stomach lurch. That lunatic Tang had fed them the story about God and it appeared that they were buying it. It was going to be hard to be nice.

"Greetings Toban! Greetings Sima!" Coda made sure to be politically correct. He merely shrugged at the Tang. Ashram hardly expected more from him. Coda only believed in himself. The conversation would go nowhere.

Toban was the first to react. He was aware of Coda. It would be tricky but he was sure he could convince him to come along. All he had to do was feed his ego.

"My dear Coda, we come to you in crisis." Sima rolled his eyes at Ashram. "Here it comes," he said.

"We have reason to believe that there will be great trouble at the edge of the universe. Apparently a being has been spotted. Now our Tang friend believes that it could be a god. However, Sima and I feel we must seek your guidance. We implore you to come with us to cast out this evilness that may come upon us."

Sima turned to Ashram and muttered, "I think I'm going to be sick."

Toban stuck his claw into Sima's side. A few deserving pokes to let him know to bite his tongue and play along. Sima looked at Coda and nodded approvingly. "You'll pay for this," he whispered.

Ashram looked into the eyes of Coda pleadingly. He knew if he played along the ego-based fish would come. It was inevitable.

Knowing he was being had, but unable to resist the flattery Coda replied, "Why of course I'll come. It is my duty to eradicate all evil from our universe. Let us be off to see what the Tang has found."

22

Ego Trumps Evil... or Perhaps Creates It

The little group arrived with divided interest. Sima and Toban anticipated a revelation. Both wished that the Tang was right. It would be a fulfillment of their deepest premonitions if this all were true. Ashram was jubilant but afraid. The combination of emotions was making him sick. What if he had imagined the whole thing? He would be an outcast forever.

Coda was beginning to feel fluttery. He could hardly move his fins to swim. He was hoping that this was all a hoax. If the Tang was right he could lose his position among the Living Beings. He knew he never had thought that these things were possible. He was Coda, a wise man among his peers. Only he was aware that his wisdom was not what it was cracked up to be.

The edge of the universe hit all of them square in the face. They all swam silently watching. Each moment an eternity. The pulse of the water a cushion for the unnerving they all felt.

It was Coda that broke the silence "There's nothing here. This is a waste of time. I say we leave."

"No, please wait a momen,." replied Ashram. "This is the exact spot where God appeared." Ashram pressed his nose against the edge. His eyes flickering back and forth peering into oblivion. Where was God? And why had she forsaken him?

Sima and Toban were disappointed. There was nothing there. All of their feelings of something else were bouncing back at them. There were no dimensional beings. There were no gods. There was only a stupid crab, a stupid shrimp, a coerced coda, and a lunatic Tang. The only hope now would be that Coda kept his mouth shut. And they both knew that that was impossible.

Ashram sighed. There was nothing there. Coda was already on his way back to the rocks, shaking with laughter. Soon all the Living Beings would confirm his stupidity. Not that they already did not know. It was common knowledge that Ashram was strange. The incident merely reinforced the issue. Toban and Sima were frustrated. Surely Coda could have given it a moment or two longer. In their hearts they felt that the Tang was telling the truth.

23

Connection

In that brief moment of pause
they both witnessed something they would never forget.
The fluid space they occupied seemed to part before their
eyes. Something was stirring towards the Tang. His eyes
lifted upward, were full of wonder. It appeared he was
being lifted towards heaven. Both swam closer and
strained their eyes. There was nothing there yet the
environment told a different story.

The Tang was lifted upward toward a light. His face
a luminous mask of joy. They even thought they heard
him whisper. "It's you!" Both crab and shrimp were silent
for the first time in their lives.

Ashram knew that God had arrived. Its tentacles
reaching for him were soft and fluid. He did not swim
away. His only regret was that Coda had left. He was
sure Toban and Sima were still there. He did not look. He
could not take his eyes off the vision of the god. Its eyes
like pools of fluid, similar to the ones that gave him life.

The eyes grew closer and he knew he had been lifted. Normally, he would have been frightened. However, transfixed in the eyes of God he felt strangely at home. "It's you," he whispered.

"Yes, it's me!"

"How have you been, my little friend?"

"And how is it that you can speak? You are a fish!"

A fish? The thought responded in Ashram's head but floated away as he moved closer to the god. What the god thought did not matter.

Juliet was concerned. It was odd for the shrimp and the crab to be in such close proximity. They had always appeared to be at odds with each other. Now the Tang was hovering around the side of the tank. It looked like they were all looking for something. Of course that was impossible. Juliet had had aquariums for years and none of the sea life had congregated like this before. She pressed her face closer and reached her hand down inside.

The Tang looked like he was in trouble. His eyes were opened extremely wide. She took a net and tried to scoop him up. A little more time in the sick tank might perk him up again. It worked before... maybe it would work now. He did not swim away. He just gazed into her eyes, his mouth moving. She might not have heard anything at all. It was when she lifted him from the water she heard him say "It's you". Now if she had not been looking directly at him she never would have believed it. There it was! The Tang had spoken to her. "You're a fish!" she exclaimed.

There was a smile of sorts at the edges of the fish's mouth. It was then that Juliet fully realized that the Tang was talking.

24

Denial & Acceptance

In her surprise
Juliet dropped the net. The Tang fell down to the bottom of the tank. She was certain that she had hurt him. All of the fish including the crab and the shrimp turned to look at him. Juliet could have sworn that the crab clapped his claws together. This was absurd.

Sima was pleased with the way his day was turning around. Obviously something or someone had lifted Ashram up and then dropped him to the sandy bottom. It was the most awkward move he had ever seen a Living Being make. It actually looked like he had been thrown. All of them raced to his side.

"Are you all right?" cried Toban.

"The Tang obviously has some problems," said Coda. He looked nervously upwards hoping to see nothing. In that precise moment Ashram turned to all of them and said, "Did you see her? The god is female!"

"Preposterous!" cried Coda.

All turned to Coda hoping he would just be quiet. Coda on the other hand felt his hold on his notoriety slipping away. In desperation, he continued to babble endlessly about his own "experience with God".

Toban and Sima rolled their eyes in unison. They were eager to hear everything Ashram had to say. It was decided that Ashram was obviously the only one who could interact with this being. The two wise shells suggested some questions that should be asked the next time that Ashram saw God.

By the time Coda finished, the others had turned back to the place Ashram had been. Toban and Sima tried in vain to see the being. The others eventually swam away, once again confused about Ashram's sanity. After all, there was nothing there. The crab and the shrimp had a vivid view of what they now referred to as the goddess.

Their belief in Ashram and his abilities increased. Toban started a list of questions in hopes that Ashram might be able to answer them through the goddess. Toban and Sima argued endlessly about the content of the questions. Coda was the only one who thought they should just go home.

Merka crept back to the group meekly. His feelings of guilt over his abandonment of Ashram filled him with great shame. Ashram just wanted to keep the goddess in his eye line. The more he saw her the more he fell in love with her. He understood her movements. The eyes translated another existence he never thought possible. Here was proof of another realm of existence. Whether she was a god or just another Living Being somehow did not matter. She was his connection to another existence. In his interactions with her he became more.

25

Total Alignment of All

Locking eyes with her
Ashram felt the bickering of Sima and Toban, the manipulations of Coda and the clinging of Merka fade away. All that was left was the goddess and the rhythmic tones she was displaying to him. Oddly, he felt a great understanding of what she was saying. The word "human" became visible and he understood. She was a goddess of sorts but she did not consider herself one. She was a life form same as he. In their chance meeting a layer of misunderstanding had been lifted and they connected, as probably they never could have under different circumstances. It was exciting. It was fragile. The best thing was that it happened. Her name was Juliet. How melodic it sounded. The vibration playing off the senses of a fish who never knew such wonders. What a lucky moment. Ashram felt a blessing so deep he almost imploded with humility. The odd Tang, now a pioneer to a new understanding. Ashram shivered at the thought.

Juliet shook her head in amazement. The Tang's name was Ashram. He thought she was a goddess. A quiver of excitement went through her. She was communicating with a fish. His eyes looking deeply into hers. An understanding filling them with something she never saw before. Her own existence faded away until she and the Tang were the only ones left. Somehow information was exchanged and a conversation ensued.

She learned all about Sima, Toban, Coda and Merka. In return Ashram learned all about the world of Juliet. The warmth of their conversation surpassing anything either of them had ever known. It was a miracle. There was no explaining. It just was.

Lost to his friends in conversation, they began to fidget. There was not a one of them who could see or hear who Ashram was talking to. Normally they would have thought it was just another episode. Somehow this was different. The look of rapture upon his face caused them to think twice.

Sima broke the silence with a "now what?" No one spoke. Each had an opinion of the moment.

Merka was in awe. He knew his friend was great, but this was unreal. He swam speechless, waiting for the next thing.

Sima was anxious to find out exactly what Ashram was seeing. He wanted to compare his thoughts with him. Impatiently he waited for the episode to be finished. He wanted answers.

Toban was squinting his eyes, trying to see. He was irritated. He considered himself evolved and the mere hint of anything less was unacceptable. He wasn't interested in comparing notes with the Tang. He wanted to experience it for himself. Why had he not been chosen?

Coda was beside himself. He saw the life that he had built for himself dissipating brick by brick. The stupid Tang was about to usurp his position. He was the chosen! He alone had seen God! His own creations embellishing his actual experiences.   He began to plot against the Tang. There must be a way to get rid of him!

26

Evolvement

Ashram and Juliet felt the world reducing until it was just the two of them. The thoughts raced back and forth as they explored this possibility of communication. Each had had a preconceived perception of the other that was incorrect.

Juliet was not a god. She was what was called a 'human being", her existence very different but just as valid as the Tang's.

Ashram was more than a fish in an aquarium. He considered his existence just as complex as Juliet's.

During their conversation they each realized their differences but also the similarities. Ashram could barely contain himself... not wanting their conversation to end but very anxious to share with his friends.

Juliet was finally called away by her parents. She promised to return right after dinner. As she bounded into the kitchen she was full of Ashram stories. Of course her parents did not believe her. They thought she had been carried away by a daydream. Certainly the fish in her tank were not talking to her. They listened with mild interest but soon their minds were filled with thoughts of their own day.

27

Back to the Sand

Ashram swam back to his friends in a state of frenzy. He did not know where to begin. He looked from Merka to Coda. What could he tell them?

Sima was the first to speak. "Well, what happened?" Toban chimed in with "Either you were talking to God or yourself. Whatever which way it was, you certainly are not a normal guy."

Merka was not sure what to do for his friend. He was worried that Ashram was indeed out of his mind. There had been no one throughout his conversation. And hearing the entire one-sided dialogue had thrown him a curve he was not ready for. He let out a sigh while shaking his head. "Tell me I'm blind Ashram. Just don't tell me you were talking to yourself. I don't think I could take the disappointment."

Ashram looked Merka square in the eye. "You are blind Merka. Better yet, there's more than a god you are not seeing. There's a whole universe out there. It's just as valid as this, only extremely different."

Merka swallowed deeply. His friend was sounding like a lunatic. The basic fiber that held his world together was unraveling. He wanted desperately to tell Ashram that his only wish was to see the vision that his friend had seen. Perhaps then he could look at his friend and believe him. Until then there would be doubt. Unable to hide his feelings, Merka swam away. Embarrassed and confused, he hid in the rocks pondering what to do.

Sima the crab crawled briskly to the center of the group. His eyes fixed on the spot where Ashram had been speaking. Aggravated by his lack of perception, he saw no reason for diplomacy.

"So Ashram, if it is not God, then who is it?"

"Juliet", replied Ashram.

"Juliet! What kind of reference is that?" cried Sima.

Toban had been standing very still. His antennae waving through the water ripples. Normally sensitive, he searched for clues to substantiate the Tang's claims. At the end of the universe there was definitely a wall. Beyond that he felt nothing. It was though the edge of the world dropped abruptly to a bottomless pit. There was nothing. Was the Tang crazy or did he really communicate with something? Toban did not know.

Sima was livid. He hoped Toban would offer some sage wisdom. Instead he was hovering about doing absolutely nothing. His claims of "sensing" wearing thin on the crab. The need for substantiation was crucial. Didn't Toban know that? As usual, Sima was left to fix the situation. It really ticked him off.

Coda had been still until now. The demise of his life had run its course through his imagination. Snapping back to the moment, he resolved to put an end to the idle rantings of the Tang. He wouldn't allow this upstart to ruin his life plan. He listened carefully while devising a method of disposal.

He knew the only way to get rid of the Tang was through natural means. It would serve him better to have the Tang die mysteriously and "most importantly" at the hand of God. Coda could then swoop in and interpret the meaning of the god's wrath and reclaim his position as the premier communicator for the Living Beings. It was perfect. Looking up, Coda saw his opportunity. The black humming box loomed ominously above him. It had been known to pronounce judgment upon those who had angered the gods. Now all he had to do was to lure Ashram there. His eyes glistened with anticipation as he planned his new ascension to power.

28

Plans for the Future

Ashram was tired.
The day had been filled with amazing events. The interaction with Juliet had left him breathless and filled with longing for their next conversation. His mind swirled with what she had told him. Hovering in the water he looked about his world with a new vision. Gone was the blind acceptance he had adhered to in the past. The stories the elders told were merely fairy tales imagined by previous elders who thought the rest of the Living Beings were stupid. Either that... or perhaps they were just unaware. They concocted the stories to explain their world to themselves. Things would be different now. He had been to the other side of the universe.

The gods were other life forms from a different origin. Imagine! Breathing air! He could not quite understand the concept. Juliet had, however, completely understood his breathing of water. She seemed so at ease with the information. He only hoped he would come to understand her existence more. This was such a huge step for the Living Beings. If only they could experience it for themselves. He knew they did not believe him. It was fine with him. Tomorrow he would tell them his plans. He hoped that they would support him.

Ashram glanced at Merka... his faithful friend. He knew that he had scared him to death this day. Still, he followed closely at Ashram's side. The true meaning of friendship conveyed in a single nod from Merka. Ashram knew he was blessed with quite a bit. Now all he had to do was to continue to spread the truth. The Living Beings were no longer alone. There were others... and there was more.

Coda lurked in the shadows. Nestled behind a sprig of seaweed he watched the two friends swim by. The smug looks on their faces sickened him. How dare they think they knew it all. How do we know he's telling the truth? No one had seen anything. Even his dumb friend Merka had swum away. Now here he was back acting like everything was fine. Certainly it was a scam of some sort. Coda knew all about scams. All Coda had to do was get rid of him. He took a deep breath and swam warmly toward the duo. His smile sparkled as he extended his fin in friendship. "This was going to be easy," thought Coda.

29

Juliet

Juliet knew that her parents did not believe her. She loved them dearly but she always knew that they did not understand her. Sometimes she felt like the grown up in their relationship.

Of course her Dad was always available for projects of interest, which included the salt water tank. He was more like her than her mother who was often extremely involved in her work.

The difference between them was a result of focus. Juliet needed everything to be crisp and clean. Dad got that. Her mother did not comprehend this idea at all.

So Juliet finished her meal with them quietly…a sense of emergency to return to the tank overwhelming her. As she gobbled down dinner, she paused to smile at the parents who didn't get that she had spoken to the little Tang in the water.

With the last gulp of milk she excused herself and made her way quickly back to her room. Hopefully the Tang would be waiting. If not, she planned on camping out until he returned.

Juliet peered into the tank while the population went about its daily ritual. All of the fish appeared to be adapting to the new chemical alignments within the tank. A thoughtful sigh passed her pursed lips as she watched the air bubbles ascend to the surface.

The Tang hovered at the rim, its eyes darting in a meticulous fashion. The idea that it had a cognitive moment similar to her own still left Juliet reeling from the idea. Imagine a fish that realized the simple complexities of life outside the tank. Obviously it was not meant to be. Obviously it was a figment of imagination meant to be a provocative thought… not an actual reality.

Ashram and Merka hovered next to the edge of the universe with anticipation. Each with a totally different agenda. They circled each other as Ashram peered into nothing.

Merka was getting tired. These past few days had depleted him of much energy.   All this talk of a goddess going over his head, but his loyalty to Ashram superseding it all. It was, however, a great amount of exertion for such a little fish. Merka didn't know how much more he could take.

Ashram continued to focus on the edge, hoping to the goddess to re-appear. He was glad that Merka was with him.   It made him feel less isolated, although he knew that his friend doubted his sanity. He loved that Merka stayed, regardless of what he believed.

As they circled in the water Coda suddenly arrived on the scene with his ever hypnotic smile.   Ashram could see Merka succumb to his charms before Coda ever opened his mouth. Ashram knew it was trouble. He just didn't know how much.

"Greetings Ashram," cried Coda as he approached. He did not feel the need to address Merka as he considered him to be of lesser stature.

"Waiting for the goddess are we?"

"Why, yes. We are," replied Ashram. Already he could sense a sinister quality to Coda's approach. He just could not identify the intent.

"I thought," said Coda, "that we could search for the goddess together. Perhaps my evolved status could help you connect with her in a more transcended fashion. You know I have experience with such things. After all, I am an ordained reverend for the Living Beings. Let me guide you."

Coda extended his fin in friendship. Ashram was hesitant but Merka was delighted in the recognition extended to the two of them.

"Sure!" he replied, swimming toward the Coda.

"No wait!" cried Ashram, but it was already too late. Merka was shrouded under the fin of the Reverend. He smiled over his shoulder to Ashram.

"Come on Ashram, we're sure to find the goddess now."

30

Betrayal

They swam upwards toward the black box of giving. Ashram hesitated but he was worried about Merka. Coda had the ability to turn one's head with his smooth talk. It was doubtful he could help them in finding the goddess. Ashram knew that and he suspected that Coda knew it as well. He swam after them knowing that he needed to rescue the ever naive Merka from his clutches.

"I'm coming Merka, wait for me."

With that Coda moved also towards the black box of giving. He would placate Ashram and then get rid of him. Obviously he had no idea where the goddess could be, he just wanted to take the credit.

So it was that the three fish moved towards the filter. Juliet watched in fascination as she observed the trio.

What were they doing?

She pressed her face close to the glass as she watched in horror as the Coda seemed to be pushing the other two fish into the motor of the filter.

31

Coda felt a flutter of fear
deep within his heart. It wasn't his nature to spin a death wish to others. He was, however, completely overwhelmed with the idea of losing his continued control over his life.

Throughout it all he had maintained an integrity through his spiritual elevation from the others. If the masses did not believe his superiority all would be lost... his position, the calm of mass reality, and the spectrum of spirituality that supported his delusional place in the hierarchy of existence. Without it, what would become of him? Or the universe?

What indeed.

With a final thrust of delusion he pushed the Tang and Merka towards the void of the giving box, hoping for an intercession from a higher perspective. Certainly his view of the world was the correct one. This Tang was only trouble. How dare he proclaim a parallel reality where he was not a dominant feature?

It was a relief to send them to their ultimate demise. There needed to be order to reality. To think there was participation of a different focus would only serve to confuse the common order of life, while Coda himself was of a higher order.

The final push was a relief. Finally all would be restored to its rightful place. The hum of the world he knew would be restored.

The execution was needed. His exoneration would be pardoned by the true nature of things.

The swoosh of energy propelled the two victims towards infinity and out of Coda's path once and for all. Their faces indicated they knew it too. A sigh of relief from deep inside came from Coda. In that final moment, however, came the hand of the goddess foretold by a simple Tang of no importance who channeled an energy that changed everything.

32

The End and The Beginning

"Curses!", cried the Coda, his surprise by the backlash created by the hand of the goddess who intercepted the Tang and Merka causing Coda himself to be sucked into the box of giving... his cries muffled by the hum of the masses who had no idea of what had occurred.

Nor did they care.

All was the same to them, the continuous circle of swimming encompassing their every thought. Drama upon drama, they continued to swim, not knowing how close they had been to disaster.

Juliet acted in impulse when she saw her favorite Tang about to be sucked into the filter. Her mind could hardly comprehend that a Coda had enough focus to push two unsuspecting fish in a hazardous area. How could that be?

On impulse, she pushed the Tang and the smaller fish out of the harm of the filter. In doing so the Coda became caught in the under current of the water and he disappeared into the filter to be seen no more.

Juliet was upset but in the same breath relieved that the cute Tang appeared to survive. In fact it looked like it was comforting the other fish. "Unreal!" she thought. "Unreal!

33

Ashram

The hand of God reached out of nowhere to save the Tang and his friend from oblivion... the black box growing smaller until they both landed on the sand of the Known Universe.

Ashram extended his fins to Merka who had landed uncomfortably on his back. In the confusion, it dawned on Ashram that somehow the Juliet had spared him from the end of existence and given he and his friend another opportunity. Somehow the experience strengthened the ties with the goddess and had given Ashram a new perspective.

Seeing that Merka was safe as well only enriched the experience, giving him a stronger sense of bonding from what he now perceived as other dimensions.

Ashram looked around the universe seeing that everything was still the same. The Chromis still swam together seeing nothing but what they wanted to see. The anemones were thinking collectively, all participating in the same circle of thought endlessly, as were most of the other inhabitants known as the Living Beings.

Sima and Toban went about their singular thoughts but now with a new found respect for him... Ashram Tang.... Merka a new convert and project for the colorful Tang. There was hope that someday Merka would see God as well.

So, Ashram was fulfilled. The opinion of the others were no longer important. He had the Juliet and a new perspective. Who knew where it would take him?

34

Juliet

It had been a long day. The Tang had survived the attempted destruction by the Coda. She had told her parents who listened with amusement to the child they believed lived in a fantasy.

They listened and then forgot as they entered their own creations. Simply, it was not the time for them to understand.

Juliet lay in her bed looking out the window at the edge of her universe. The stars were twinkling, a full moon had traveled across the sky and centered itself in her view. The idea of the vastness of existence piqued her ever continuous questions about everything.

"What if?" she thought.

"What if I reached into the sky and found a god? What if I realized that he saw me and I could have a conversation like the Tang did with me?"

"What if it were true?"

Juliet pulled her blanket to her chin and glanced at her saltwater tank. She saw the Tang hovering at the edge of his world... just as she was.

"I wonder how far this goes?" she thought, just before she drifted off to her dreams.

The Crab Sima inched his way along foraging the stone wall, thinking deeply about the foraging job at hand. He was no longer disappointed in life... evolving existence now a choice for whomever desired it available.

Sima was at last satisfied.

Toban looked toward Sima with new hope. Perhaps they could align now in this new energy or at least feel the hope now available for all. Toban closed his eyes then reopened them to a new time and place.

Toban was at last fulfilled.

The fish all continued their daily circle of life. A small group of Chromis darted through the maze of definition they called their universe, however, now instead of a circle, they swam in a straight line to the edge of the universe.

What would happen now?

Sima and Toban could hardly wait.

***

"Reflections"

"Anytime there is growth in the spirit, there is joy throughout the cosmos..."

"Rainbows are an

orchestration of the inner soul

of nature. Create rainbows of

your inner self. Others

appreaciate the splendor.

Allow your colors to

show..."

*"The Warmth of spiritual

contact is delectable..."*

"Friendship is an agreement, made between souls, to support and hold above all others..."

"One must ready oneself to accept all levels of emotion to be a friend: Not an easy task..."

"The sum of our actions allow for infinite possibilities, limited only to our wildest imagination and deepest desire..."

"Physical connections wither, as physical does. Spiritual is forever..."

CHOICE

"Choice is the power to select.

To choose is to have power..."

"An era of possibilities present themselves to those with a hunger for the infinite..."

"Manifestation comes from release, not clinging..."

"Jealousy is a process which occurs when one is actually dissatisfied with his or her own creations..."

"What you create in your life is usually balance by what you put into it..."

"*Prosperity begins when you*

lose your fear of yourself..."

"Be bold when the

opportunity presents itself..."

TRUST

"While it is admirable to question all that is around you, there is something to be said for trust. It is a special gift: Given by few... to few..."

"Fear is the true root of all mishap..."

"You will never miss fear

once it's gone..."

"Only in taking a step does one begin to fulfill their destiny..."

"How do you become a pure soul? Drink of truth in all things in life..."

"The fine line between arrogance and confidence is Truth..."

"*Awareness is a treasure...*"

"Security is being at peace with

one's own self identity..."

"It takes courage to be self aware..."

"Don't look behind you for what you want in front of you.... for what is behind you usually wants to grab on and keep you there with it..."

"Life – Fear = Evolution..."

Life

- Fear

Evolution

"Life

minus Fear

equals Evolution..."

"Evolution does not mean you are stepping up. It means you are stepping out and expanding...

"If you haven't guessed I'll give you a clue, the master of the universe is inside of you..."

xxx